LOVE + ANGST

THE COMPLETE 80'S POETRY COLLECTION

Carol Killman

The Book Couple • Boca Raton, FL

Published by
The Book Couple
Boca Raton, FL 33433
www.thebookcouple.com

© 1990, 2010, 2016 Carol Killman Rosenberg
ISBN-13: 978-0-9908458-3-6

AUTHOR'S NOTE

I offer no apologies for this poetry, although
I probably should (most especially to myself).
I was an angst-ridden teenager in the 80s,
searching for something outside myself that
I'd never find. A lot of this poetry sucks (really,
it does, and that's okay), but there are
a few gems hidden among the rocks.
(You'll have to bring your own chisel,
especially if one of the poems appears
more than once, which is *very* likely.)

Read at your own discretion.
I just wanted to put this book on my shelf
and be done with it, you know, for that angst-
ridden teenager who would probably think it's
totally cool that all her poetry is in a book on
someone's shelf, even if it's her own shelf.

—Carol Killman Rosenberg
January 2017

CONTENTS

THE STRANGLED LIFE WORTH LIVING

I wonder why.

Oh, I just wonder why.
Every so often, I just sit
down and wonder,
Why?

A pen cap

chewed on in deep creative thought
has disappeared forever to the lonely
land of stray
pen caps.
Neither I, nor my favorite blue pen
can survive without the
pen cap.
Now that my beloved
pen cap
no longer rests upon the tip of
my favorite blue pen,
the ink has dried up
like a creek in a drought.
No longer do I need a
pen cap
. . . or paper
. . . or thoughts.

Time is going by

much too fast,
it slips through the hourglass,
leaving the present
in the past.
The little children are now
old and gray,
they rock away time
no longer do they play.
The mighty oak tree
will wither and die,
as the gray blanket
covers the sky.
Time goes by too quickly for us,
we're no longer here,
just piles of dust.

A flower unlike any other

has been plucked from
the shallow earth.
Its petals so silky
smooth and violet
bring tears to my eyes
to know
that it is no longer alive
Twas a flower so rare
like a gift from the Gods
One to feast your eyes on
and one that lends
you its fragrance each
time you sniff it.
Twas a beautiful flower
one which may never grow again
for this one has been picked
put in a vase
left there only to shrivel
away into nothing
leaving only in its place
a dead stringy thing.

Part of me floats above

the clouds in a fantasy
the other part remains
close to the ground
to be stepped on
by the foot of reality.
I am somewhere in between.

Here I sit behind this desk

my mind forever wanders.
Is there a purpose for all of this?
It's a question on which I often ponder.
I wasn't meant for filing,
nor stamping cards and such.
At this desk in this office
of reality I've lost touch.
The windows are bright,
the sun shines through.
Out there there's another world
for which I am blue.
The time goes by too quickly.
My life is passing away.
I watch it go, but sometimes,
it seems as if I missed a day.
Out the window I see a world
in which part I belong
I do not know.
But out there, I know there's
somewhere that I must go.

Too much love

Too much understanding
Too much sharing
Too much caring
. . . is it possible?

The sky is filled with a thousand stars

there just for you and me
It's as if the sun appears
just so we can see.

Tis a midnight sky I see

as I stare out the window
at the darkness before me
devouring me with its vastness
feeling insignificant in a space that never ends
in a place that knows no boundaries.

Away

I'm flying away
above the sky
please do not cry
light
It's so warm
peaceful
the light is blinding me
oh so bright
please have no fright
Away
I'm flying away
above the sky
please do not cry.

A castle of magnificence,

painstakingly built
stone by stone.
The drawbridge is up.
Travelers unwelcome.
No one to greet them
for they are all gone.
The main hall rings not
with the sounds of the past.
The kitchens add no clattering
of pans, to the silence.
Deathly stillness emits an
obnoxious odor throughout
the magnificent rooms.
And the bones of a child
lay scattered on the damp floor
the only clue that we were
once here and destroyed
the world for our children.

All of the flowers are dying.

Someone had better remind God
to buy Mother Nature
another bouquet.

A box: what's in the box?

Life: what's going to happen?
Open the box and you shall find out.

Be by my side

for there are places to visit
worlds to explore
people to love.

Listen. . .

Can you hear him?
Can you hear him crying?
Tears falling from the sky,
Oh God, why have we made you cry?

"I"

I am trapped,
I can grieve.
I can't forgive,
I could've forgotten.
I don't want to lose you
I gaze out the window
(I knew you'd be back),
I know how to play!
I lose myself. . .
I searched for you.
I wish it were summer,
I'll be the one to cry.
I'm through!
In the cold misty fog,
In the depths of your eyes,
Is it you?
Is this the end?
It is not.
It's turned into a nightmare
I've finally come to terms.

One person in the whole world.

Imagine.
Where has everyone gone to?
Where are all the children?
the trees? the birds?
What have we done?
What shall we do?
Imagine.

Reincarnation:

The candle is burning.
The candle is burnt out.
Use the wax to mold a new candle.

The world is forever changing

Mountains rise, valleys form
People die and new life is born
Lightning cracks and hits a tree
a limb tumbles to the grass
and burns till it is ash.

Could it be like floating

through the mist
on a sapphire cloud?

In what place have I arrived?
Form what world did I come?
Has night devoured day?

Just a twinkle of light would
be welcome here,
in this deep dark dimension.

Just a ray of sun. . . and no more darkness
Just a smile . . . and no more foe.

In what place have I arrived?
From what world have I come?
Where is this sapphire cloud taking me?

Darkening skies

open up to devour your mind
dreading tomorrow
visions of dawn
stored away deeply
missing yesterday
pain heartache loneliness

Maybe this time. . .

I say
Maybe next time,
I say, again
No never, I decide.

. . . the same routine

morning after morning . . .

Rise at dawn.
Train by 7:02.
Every minute counts,
Rush.
Step over people sleeping on the floor.
Pay no attention.
Every minute counts.
The same routine
morning after morning
people passing
pushing by
nobody attempting to help the poor
out for themselves
living as the minute hand moves.

Outside the window

I see the world,
in which I cannot belong
Has God made a mistake
in placing me in the strange cold world
or is my own mind mistaken
by wishing for untamed
mountains in place
of the hollow structures
outside my window?

Why does the sun only shine

on sunny days?
Why does it rain
only when rain drops fall?

Do not let tomorrow frighten you

for it is not there
to make you suffer
It is there to let you live another day

Dreams:

Are they futuristic events
that will take place in just a short time?
Or are they fragments
of what's been left over in our minds?

I Wish It Were Summer

The ground is covered
with a large white blanket.
From the sky falls
tiny white balls.
The trees sway back and forth
with the strong, cold wind
and I wish it were summer again. . .

The sun sets and leaves
a cool breeze over the beach.
The tide is high,
as the moon grows stronger.
The sand settles down with
the setting of the wind.
And I am glad that it is
summer again . . .

The ground is covered
with a large white blanket.
From the sky falls
tiny white balls.
The trees sway back and forth
with the strong, cold wind
and I wish it were summer again. . .

Do you believe in fantasies?

dreams of another kind
where illusions are the keys
to unlock one's mind?

I may not be terrific,

I may not be peachy keen,
But all I know,
is that I am,
somewhere in between!

In the cold misty fog

I ran.
Down the corridors of life
I ran.
Through the stars and space
I ran.
Through the glistening stream
I ran.
Through the green green meadows
I ran.
On the roughest of surfaces
I ran.
Over the highest mountain
I ran.
Across the desert sand
I ran.
Around the world
I ran.
I ran.
I ran I am free.

If I could only change

the way things had to happen
I'd change them into rainbows
and light which never dims.

I'm lost in my dreams

Somewhere far away from here
Where no mortal man can find me
I stare into space
But what I see before me
is not what lies within my gaze
I see a world different than our own
I see a future bright and clear
I see the present
(unfinished)

It just can't be

there's more to life
than our day-to-day routine
There are so many wonderful things
from birth to death . . .
there's so much in between
Maybe we don't understand
Why God chose to put in this place
let our questions go unanswered
and for the time
We must have faith

In a world where there is
so much hatred,

In a world where there is so much sadness,
In a world where there is so much greed,
I have found true love.

I've found the meaning of happiness.
I've found the joy of living.
I have found the answers.
I've found the reason for being.
I have found true love.

In a world where there are so many questions,
In a world where the answers are impossible to find,
I have found true love.

In a world where unkindness
flows like a river in a flood,
In a world where hunger and thirst run on for miles
I've found understanding.
I've found the words that make living
    a little easier.
I've found true love.

In a world where the future is so uncertain;
In a world where death and destruction live on,
I've found a tomorrow.
I've found a creative mind.
I've found true love.

In a world that knows no honesty
In a world that knows no trust
In a world that has no faith
I have found true love.
I've found the nobleness of centuries
I've found the hidden truths
I've found what it is to have faith.
I have found true love.

In a world where there is emptiness
In a world where there is loneliness
In a world where there is boredom
I have found you.

Because I Care

I care about you
more than you know,
wherever you are
that's where I'll go.
If you need my help
or just want to talk,
let me know where you are
and that's where I'll walk.

If you ever need someone
and want them to care,
call out my name and
I'll be there.

If you are ever lonely
and need someone to hold,
call out my name
'cause I fit your mold.

If you ever grow weak
and can no longer stand
reach out to me
and I'll give you my hand
. . . because I care.

It hasn't snowed yet.

Thank God for that.
I hate getting hurt.

I haven't fallen in love yet.
Thank God for that.
I hate wearing boots.

Jealousy

The green eyed monster
has taken reign
only to add
more heartache and pain.

She lurks in the darkness
her eyes glow bright
struggling and sobbing,
she puts up a fight.

You may not know her
from just one view
for she wears a mask
that seems bold and true.

Before you know it,
she gets a hold of your life
and turns everything wrong
even before it was right.

Beware when you turn
for it's not the wrong way,
you may bump into jealousy
then she's there to stay.

Wicked Smile and Charm

I'll never forget
her wicked smile or charm
or her devilish eyes
that could only bring harm.
Her harsh cruel words
were nothing but profane,
her actions were worse
simply, she was untame.
I hate her face
and I must not lie,
I wish she'd wither away,
drop dead and die.

Memories all piled together

in a box
masking tape sealing them away
from probing eyes
in the back of my closet
in the back of my mind
Some were wonderful
others so painful
I wonder, had I stored them away
to keep them safe from others
or from myself?

No I don't talk much

I've always preferred to listen
but nobody understood.
So I decided to add to a conversation once,
and nobody understood.

Somewhere deep inside,

hidden for centuries
in the depths of the Creator's mind,
we were there
. . . already laughing
. . . already loving
And when you entered this new world
    before I,
you were lost
and I lost without you,
but not ready to begin life.

When finally the Creator
let me slip from his mind,
I was tossed into a life
so different than yours
that our ever meeting again,
loving again,
was almost impossible.

In your search for the soul
that you'd known,
you'd mistaken it for another
and you were unhappy
 as was I
for I knew that you were
somewhere out there,
so far from my reach.

Two unhappy souls,
the Creator saw then
and knew his mistake.
He commanded destiny to step in
and we were reunited
no doubt in our minds
that we belonged together
as we had been for centuries
. . . laughing and loving.

Someone's Nightmare (Life)

Sleeping peacefully
in a far away place
no revealing expressions
on his face.
He lies there dreaming,
dreaming on
watching the lives
of the here and gone.
Would you please awake
from the long and dreary night
and put a stop to our unending fright?
Do you sleep just to watch us cry?
To see us enter your dream, then die?
It is your nightmare
but please wake up,
I'm a part of it
and I want it to stop.

The dark street

the silent night
the people crying
the people dying
a cloud of sorrow covers the earth.
The dark shadows in the room
the dead lying in the grave.

The feel of your body

close to mine
brings me far away
to a fantasy shrine.

The candle of time

is burning down
will it end
without a sound. . .
or will man extinguish the flame?

Time . . .

Life . . .
People . . .
Together . . .
Joy . . .
Sharing . . .
Caring . . .
Love . . .
You . . .
me . . .

The sun shines its brightest

when your eyes reflect its light
and I no longer feel the need
to cry during the dim hours of the night.

The moon glows its strongest,
when I'm gazing at it with you
At the arrival of the first sign of day
I'm no longer feeling blue.

There is no answer

I can give
no facts to soothe the mind
I do believe
they're deep inside
But those answers we must find.
Life sometimes seems
so trivial
We wonder why we're here
but we must remember
there is a purpose
for every smile or tear.
The world can be so
cruel at times
People can cause much pain
but we must remember
that sunshine
will always follow the rain.
Life sometimes seems like
a struggle to get by
to survive
Often I find myself wondering
    if this is the only reason
we're alive.

They are his invisible children

Our less fortunate brothers
the ones we do not see
those we take for granted
as we would take for granted
a lamppost or street sign
Those who are truly in need
those God has put there to test us
begging with their eyes
Yet we do not see them
blocked from our mind
should we stumble upon one in our haste
nothing we can do
Yet if we had the time
the money
the way
there'd be so much we would do.
Yet the thought fades
as quickly as it had come
and it is forgotten
which we take for granted
all that we have
the beings that we are
They are his children
Our brothers
These people of the street
Sorry souls
His invisible children.

12/87

Tomorrow

Another day approaches.
Let us remember
the gifts God gave;
Let us not be blind.

There are so many thoughts in my mind,
but I can't set them free . . .
either that,
or they don't want to be.

The clock says time's going by too fast

because I'm always waiting for tomorrow,
always anticipating the future,
ignoring the present.
What happens when the future becomes
    the present?
Will I have waited my whole life away?

The light's out

and the music's on.
I lie in bed,
all problems gone.
Where's my mind?
It's drifting away,
forgetting the bad thoughts
letting the good stay.
Lying in bed
all alone
just hearing the music,
then the ringing of the phone.
The music's off
and the lights are on.
Where are all the peaceful thoughts?
Where have they gone?

I ask myself over and over again why?

Why do I do this to myself?
There's really no answer.
One day everything will be going great.
Too great for me and then all of a sudden bam!
    Things hit me like a bolt of lightning.
I do it to myself though. I make problems.
I don't know why I do that.
Is there something wrong with me?
Do I make problems,
because I thrive on them?

DOOMED LOVE
FROM SUNRISE

Don't let me fall

in love with you,
for in a few short weeks,
it'll all be through.

My lips await your in a neverending wait.

The Meaningful Kiss

He'll hold your hand and won't let go
he'll tell you he loves you but you already know.
His heart'll beat fast, yours will too
It's then you know he's going to kiss you.
You'll swallow hard and wet your lips
you'll look up slowly and tell him you're his.
Your eyes will meet, then you'll look away
you'll close your lids and begin to pray.
Slowly he touches your hair and face
your heart will beat at an irregular pace.
Your lips'll meet, all thoughts will stop
your bodies'll be entangled
    and your hearts will drop.
Your lips'll be together, you'll want more and more
it's almost as though, you've never kissed him
    before.

Always and Forever

Always and Forever
are two simple words
that stand for so much,
Though they and reality,
may never quite touch.

Always seems so certain,
like the rain in the spring.
And Forever seems so lasting,
like the diamond in a ring.

When I say Always and Forever, dear,
I only mean to say
that I'm Certain our love will Last,
for more than just today.

With Someone Just Like You

I WANT TO SHUFFLE
through the fallen leaves,
beneath the stars
and under the trees.

I WANT TO DREAM
of unicorns,
of mystic forests,
of fiery dawns.

I WANT TO SAIL
across oceans of blue
and tame that mighty dragon,
which St. George slew.

I WANT TO WALK
down the hallway of life
and open every door.

I WANT TO COLLECT
the rarest of shells
from foreign sandy shores.

I WANT TO CHASE
my shadow around
and catch it in my grasp.

I WANT TO LISTEN
to the unfamiliar sounds
from the world's distant past.

I WANT TO BE
a little girl
in a wonderland of places

I WANT TO VISIT
a world above the clouds
and see old familiar faces.

I want to do this all,
with someone bold and true.

I WANT TO DO THIS ALL,
WITH SOMEONE JUST LIKE YOU.

My dreams are filled with future

Who knows what will happen
I can assure you neither you nor I
so we'll see what may be
Who knows what will happen
neither you nor I can tell
what may be, but for the time
I'd like you to know,
that you mean so much to me.

Before You Leave

Can I have
a kiss goodnight?
Before you leave,
hold me tight.
Tell me how you feel
one more time,
let me know
you're really mine.
Hold me close
and let me know,
that if you didn't have to,
you'd never let me go.
Whisper sweet nothings
into my ear,
tell me the things
that I like to hear.
Say so long,
'cause it's never goodbye,
the sun has set
the moon's in the sky.
So, can I have
a kiss goodnight,
just to let me know
everything's alright?

I do not want you to unlock my heart.

So please, don't even bother knocking.

Love is a word

so complicated
so involved
a word that is impossible
to understand completely
Does it have just one meaning?
Does it have any meaning at all?
When it happens
can you feel it?
Do you know for sure that this
is the one true love of your life,
just as all the rest were supposed to be?
When it happens
will you feel more pain
than happiness?

Words are so hard to come by

when one feels as I do
In just a short time
I've found something
    so special in you.

My thoughts drift to and fro
from here and to there
but they are always of you
because I've grown to care.

You're a masterpiece in my mind
outshining the sun's bright rays
there's so much I want to share
in so many different ways.

You came into my life
bringing along
all that I ever wished
the softness of your hands
and gentleness of your kiss.

I want to let everything go
and hold you so very near
but I am so frightened
for I know
you may not always be here

Don't promise me anything
or tell me of your fantasies and dreams
unless all that you say
is everything that you mean.

And if you find fault
and I'm not all that you desire
let me know soon
for I may fall too quickly into the fire.

Your powerful embrace, your witty smile
and sharp green gaze
have already pulled me too close
in just so few days.

My darling, you're so special
and deserve all I have to bestow
I'll try my hardest to make you happy
something I can do I know.

So let's take it all very slowly
and see what may be
but for the time I'd like you to know
you mean so very much to me.

In your eyes I see

the promise never spoken
which cannot be broken nor kept
I appreciate that more than any promise
promised.

Good-bye, good-bye.

No I'll never say good-bye.
For that would mean I will
never cross your path again.
But, my love, you must understand.
We are meant for one another.
Crossing paths we will do,
time and time again.

Were we truly ever strangers?

Had we passed on the street
time and time again
and not noticed
that together there would be two of us?

Could it be that we were only friends,
for I was yearning the reach out
and touch any part of you
just to feel closer?

Is it possible that we are so different
brought up in separate worlds
my right, your wrong?

Are we in any position
have we any right to feel?

And did the gentle touch of your lips
press against my own
as my body pressed into
your warm embrace?

Where will I go?

What will I do?
If you leave me here. . .
alone.

Where will I turn?
Who will I turn to?
If you leave me here. . .
alone.

Would you be

could you be
more than a friend to me?

Would you hold me
could you hold me
close to your body?

I need you now
as more than just a friend
I'm too far gone to just pretend?

Whisper. Whisper my name...

For it feels so fitting to hear you breathe it.

Kiss my lips...
For a touch sends the blood through my veins.

Hold my hand...
For the strength in yours lends me support.

Laugh with me...
For the ringing sound delights me.

...and Love me...
For your adoration fills me with pleasure.

We were so very young

when first we fell in love
the kisses we shared
the innocent hugs.

At first they were a game
in which we both won
But we grew too fast and
the games were no longer fun.

Our feelings grew stronger
and together we shared
things that innocents
would never ever dare.

The feelings were overbearing
our emotions grew confused
There had been so much to gain
but alas so much to lose.

It was almost as if
without the other we'd die
I was a part of "You"
and you were a part of "I."

You meant so much to me
and you still do
but I'm sorry, my darling,
Can't you see we're through?

We've been together
for so many years
It's time to put into memories
the laughter and the tears.

Our lips touched

but once
and for all that I am
I wish that I hadn't let you go
I searched for something more
but little did I know
that but once should have been
the end of my search
Our lives touched but for a moment in time
and yet I feel as if I've known you forever

This feeling doesn't come along too often

Some say it's not even true
but, my darling, I've known
for some time now
that I've fallen in love with you.

Your eyes pierce through
my very soul
the feeling swells my heart
your face lingers in my mind
whenever we're apart.

There is so much

that I want to be
So much in me
that I want you to see.

I want to be all
that you desire
In your green eyes
I want to see fire.

A Spanish tigress
a lily in her hair
with long red fingernails
at your back, I would tear.

As an Amazon from the Nile
to your knees you would fall
we wouldn't speak any words
But we'd understand it all.

A child ike woman
in your strong arms I would quiver
You'd keep my young body warm,
but still I would shiver.

A beautiful peasant girl
so under your power
you'd order me to do for you
in return, I'd receive flowers.

An exotic dancer
for my caress you would yearn
veil by veil
for my body you would yearn.

As a black-eyed Indian squaw
sons I would bare
the pride in your eyes
would always be there.

A fairy-tale princess
from a never-ending story
you'd make me a queen
in all of her glory.

All of these things
I would like to be
but most of all
I want to be me.

For as me I can be
honest and so much more
but every once in a while
you won't know what's in store.

In a world where men

are no longer heroes
and chivalry has politely excused itself
and white chargers are just
another form of gambling
you came along
and made me feel like a
woman again.

The way I feel about you:

I need you.
I want you.
I love you.

The way you feel about me:
you need me.
you want me.

But where in God's name
is the love?

I need love just as much as I need you.

I Can't Forgive Myself

It seemed so wrong
and yet it was right,
having you in my arms
and holding on tight.
When I lie beside you
I feel complete
and just the thought of having you
makes my heart beat.
There were nights I'd lie awake
and dream for one to hold,
but now you're here to
shelter me from the cold.
I've been hurt many times
which has left me so afraid
searching always for the king of hearts
but turning up a spade.
You treat me with kindness
and words so dear,
but those are the words
that I most fear.
You seem so loving
so bold and true,
yet I still can't forgive myself
for falling in love with you.

Hello, love

it's me again.
It's been a while, has it not?
Do you miss me as desperately
    as I miss you?

Do you think of me often
and remember those beautiful
memories of times long gone?

Do you often wish that someday
we could be "we' again?

Do you dream at night
and wake up the next morning
and wish that dreams was true?

I do.

Hold me close

and never let me go,
because if you do,
I'll melt in the hot summer sun.

Hold me in your arms,

but not too tightly.
For if you do, when you let me go,
I might be broken.

Lay your head

down to rest,
down to rest,
Place your head upon soft pillow
close your eyes for sleep,
my love, sleep
Miss me not, my handsome prince
miss me not
Drift into your dreams
and I shall enter mine.
There we shall meet.

Once upon a poem

I spoke of a wall which I built
    brick by brick,
Never to be melted by the flames in your eyes.

I swore I had a heart of ice
    that couldn't be chiseled through.

I swore so very much,
because I saw something frigtening in you.

Love was

somewhere close at hand.
Tender years told me so.
My heart was so open, anyone could enter.

Let's be together now and forever

you be the one to hold me tight
you be the one to take away the fright
you be the one to let me love you.

Let's pretend

that we're holding hands
because that's all I need from you.
Now let's pretend that you love me
and that I love you too.

Let's listen to one another

just this once,
and we'll realize how
foolish you really do sound.

As close as my bare feet

are to the ground,
yet as far from my reach
as the midnight moon.
In the depths of the seas,
I spy myself
and my eyes are blocked with pain.
No longer can I remain your friend,
for I long to hold you in my arms
and press my lips gently against those
belonging to you.
I long to whisper my deepest secret
that I've denied too long,
and to share with you my enchanted dreams
of love forever lasting.
Never will you get as close as my feet
are to the ground,
for that would be close enough
to let me fall in love,
but you are close enough to let me
wish I could.
Can you see the longing in the depths
of my eyes?
Can you see how very much you've come
to mean to me?
Can't you see
that I've been waiting for you
Forever?

Are you truly hers to hold?

In your arms is she safe?
When you think of holding her close,
do you love her more each day?
I never meant to steal from her
those few precious times
but in those eyes I saw someone
and I knew there were moments to find.
I put her out of my thoughts
washed away that she was real
but too often I'd hear in your voice
about how much you really did feel.
Can you tear your eyes away
from the beauty that she does possess
and when you look into her eyes
is it me that you forget?
I never really envied her
for in your arms I was there too
But lately there is something more
something so very new.
I'm scared of how I feel
for I know "We" could never exist
but these feelings remain intact
In my heart they persist.
She has something so special
in you she found a treasure
one that will always be out of my reach
just a few moments of pleasure.

And yet I do not remember who
*   this poem was written about*

Are we underneath the twinkling stars

on a clear warm night
or is it only my imagination
playing tricks again
tormenting me with your tantalizing smile?

Are your strong arms beckoning me
to melt in your warm embrace
or is it just a fantasy
that returns every so often
to remind me that I am cold?

Are you whispering words of love
so that only I can hear
or is it the wind teasing me
as it blows through the leaves?

A poker game

was not what I had in mind,
but I am willing to play.
Now, if you'll be so kind,
wash your poker face away.

Can you see the cards in my eyes?
Is my smile too bright, as I'm told?
Are you going to raise the bid
or lay your cards down, fold?

Must my expressions be like yours
so unanswering and straight
What are the cards that
you have in your hands
Queen? King? an Ace?

I'm learning this game well
and never will you know
until I lay them down flat
and they're safe to show.

I'm having a problem,
small it may be,
It lies within the depth of the king,
Hearts or spades? you may ask—
I do not know, that's the thing.

Or is it?

I glanced across the room at you.
Your smile seemed to outshine the crowd.
You saw my eyes searching you
Yet a smile was glued to my face.

Is your smile as unreal as mine?

Is it there just to make me think
that you don't care and that you're having fun
    without me?
Is it there to make me feel as if I've lost you forever?

It won't work. You can't fool me.
Your smile is as unreal as mine.
. . . or is it?

Out the window I look

into the crowded but empty world
and I remember
the laughter and the love

I forget for a fleeting moment
the pain and the tears

Then suddenly it all comes back
and I yearn to erase unkind memories
from my mind

But they are there to remain
until time takes its toll.

If I say I cry sometimes over my loss
I'd be lying
but there are times
when my heart feels empty
A missing piece of the puzzle
and I'd give anything to be
in your arms

But I know I must not for
if I did I'd hurt us both . . . once again
for when reality takes its toll
I'll know that pure love
just isn't meant to be.

Our eyes met

your green gaze held mine for
the very first time
And I yearned to tell you how I felt.

You'd brush past against me
Our arms would touch
for just a moment
but waves of pleasure
would run their course.

And when we held hands for the first time
I thought my heart would stop beating.

I held my breath as you leaned over to kiss me
Afraid that if I let it go,
you would disappear into the darkness.

And when the kiss was over
and I opened my eyes
you were still there
Not only just a dream but a reality.

I can feel your strength when you hold me
I can hear the tenderness in your voice
When I'm near you, I feel protected, cherished.

I wonder if this will last only a while,
as it has so many times before.

. . . afraid to get close
. . . afraid to be hurt again
. . . afraid it is not what you want
. . . afraid of what I feel

To tell you how much
    you've come to mean to me
Unsure if I truly mean it.
Not ready, too soon.

At times I yearn
to tell you those precious words
But I am so frightened of being alone.
Would those words make you walk away?
With those words, I'd be committed.

Outside the world buzzes

cars whiz by
drivers unknown
people walk quickly
through the streets
facelessly
the wind blows
the sun shines
but the only
thing that exists
in my mind
is us
nothing else matters

Fall in love with me, please

there is nothing more that I want
than to be by your side.

Dance with me
twirl me about
like a fairy-tale princess
drowning in the love
of her fairy-tale prince

Be all to me
that I want to be for you
and love me
with all your heart

I could put up a front
and pretend not to care
Ah, but you know I do.

Being here so close to you
and yet so far,
brings tears to my eyes.

I want not what it was
but what it could have been
and know it could never be.

At first glance

I see you in the light
    of the midnight moon
and I wonder if the trees
    have always played
    this bittersweet tune.
For a man as godly
    and as worldly as thee
is confused and questions
    the very thought of me.
I have not one memory
    of the distant past
but the future holds my dream
    of being yours at last

I see a woman in the lake,
    wet and shimmering like Ivory gold
wanting to touch her
    and needing someone to hold.

But this heart of mine
    has been pricked and left sore
sworn on a grave
    that I would love no more.

A figure just a shadow
    haunts me at night
and will till the day
    the awesome feeling of love
wins the fight.

A love so strong and powerful
    that nothing can keep them apart
as hard as one will try
    You can't deny the love
 that is in their hearts.

Our time together was special

a time I shall never forget
the future without you
is all that I will regret.

It's time to say good-bye
all though it causes so much pain

Good-bye is a sad sad word. . .
remember my tears,
when it rains.

I want to be by your side

every moment that can be spared
I want to be a part of you
and share all that can be shared.

I want to whisper words of love
and hold you close to my breast
I want to fall fast asleep
upon your masculine chest.

I want you to be my handsome hero
a prince from a place afar
I want to be your lady love
beneath the moon and stars.

I want to roam about the world
my hand clenched tight with yours
and look to you adoringly
as we take our adventurous course.

I want to kiss you gently
our lips locked without a key
and be this way forever
by your side an eternity.

This poem is yours

that means for no one else
that's only because I wrote it myself.
I'm wishing you were here
and in my arms,
from my eyes fall tears,
because you are gone.
The minutes go by,
slowly they do
I sit back and cry
because I'm not with you.

A golden God

of light
with turquoise
globes of ice
A superior frame of form
with strength to rue
the strong
Limbs so firm and powerful
A sound so pleasing
to the ear
A touch so gentle it caresses
even as you look
A mind so perfect
filled with brilliance
even in sleep
but one that understands
the silence of a weep

That's what I see in him.

Are you somewhere out there

dreaming of me
as I dream of you
night after lonely night?

Are you as handsome and godly
as I imagine
and someday will you hold me
gently in your arms
and whisper words of love
in my ear?

Do you dream of us walking along
the sandy beach
hand in hand
And as the sun sets can't you almost
feel our lips touch softly?

Ah yes, my first love

it is I. . .
thinking of you.
Time and time again I do
Is it so hard to believe
that memories are still painful
that they live on in my mind?
They don't seem to fade, my first love
The years have passed
    and yet
Time seems to have stood still.

As a child,

I'm frightened
of these new overwhelming emotions

As a girl,
I am fascinated
with fresh exciting feelings

As a woman,
I am satisfied
to possess this security in my heart

As a lover,
I find that I am all of the above
Not only frightened, fascinated, and satisfied
I am bursting at the seams
with what I know is love

Could it be that we

were once strangers
In this game of life
where we're just players?

Fate dealt the cards
Friends we became
but the feelings I had
were so very strange

I was unsure, unsure
of what you thought
we're all so different, at least
that is what we were taught

We'd speak and I'd yearn
to tell you so much
wanting to touch you and
to feel your touch.

Can I share my dreams

with you
and make them yours
as I would make your
dreams mine?

Can I tell you of
my tears, secrets
and every thought I have
just as I want to know
every part of you?

Can you hold me
in your arms and
keep me there
forever?

Can we open up to
one another just this once>
For if we did, we'd see
just how wonderful
life could be.

Fallen out of Love

The times we had
were good times,
but they are all in the past.
The times to come
are not for us,
but for two people
who will last.
Little things
that bothered me not,
are beginning to show up many.
Things like that
I should ignore,
but lately I've seen plenty.
I do not see you too often,
as much as I liked to before,
absence should make the heart
grow stronger
but I don't really care anymore.
You don't seem too offended
I didn't think you would,
I'm glad I finally said something,
'cause I didn't think I should.
I know it's sad and I'm sorry,
but I'm afraid that it's true
we both saw it coming,
I've fallen out of love with you.

Has it been an eternity?

For I feel as if I've known you forever.
Was it only yesterday,
for sometimes I shiver in your presence.
Did you hold me in your arms but once
for it feels as if we have
joined time and time again.

I don't want to lose you

or say good-bye forever
for in your eyes I saw a future
and my life seemed a little better.
For in my heart I feel the pain
of your final speech
I feel the tears not yet fallen
and the love so out of reach.
I wander far and alone
wondering how things can be so wrong
when all I wanted was someone with
    whom I could truly belong.
I wanted to hold you and laugh
with you and cry
I wanted it all for ever
I wanted so hard to try.
I felt so at ease
in your strong and powerful embrace
as if I could stay there always
and that would be my place.
Misunderstandings happen so often
they confuse the mind and soul
the feelings all bunch together
in one dark empty hole.
Our time together was special
a time I shall never forget
The future without you
is all that I will regret.
It's time to say good-bye
although it causes so much pain
Good-bye is a sad sad word. . .
    remember my tears when it rains. . .

I gaze out the window

at the city below
and I know that you are somewhere out there

So out of reach but yet so close

If I close my eyes I can see your face
lips parted
eyes as bright as a clear blue sky

I can almost feel your arms
tight about me

I think back to the beginning
when our lips first met
A memory,
I am unable to erase.

I cannot tell you
what is going on in my heart
for if I do,
I might lose a very dear friend

She is so very lucky
to have you
but I do not envy her
the pain
if your love should not
persist.

My love,
You're out there somewhere
so I'll say it into the wind
Maybe it'll reach you. . .
I love you.

I lose myself in your eyes,

for they are so deep, so trusting,
so honest.

I lose myself in your arms,
for they are so strong, so warm,
so protecting.

I lose myself in your words,
for they are so tender, so meaningful,
so true.

I lose myself when I'm with you,
for your very presence radiates a true
meaningful love. . .

and then I find myself in your heart.

I've run out of words

to express my feelings
I've told you time and time again
that I love you and I do
More than anyone could understand
But even greater than those words
I love you
I have found a way to tell you
exactly what it is inside
I feel you.

I've finally come to terms

with the fact that you don't
want me.
The thoughts and memories that
forever drifted through my mind
have ceased.
The flowers are old and brittle
the pictures are safely tucked
far away
my days are just as they
were before, my mind
on more important things.
But at night, in my dreams
your memory haunts my
every sleeping minute.
In my dreams you are
everything you were,
everything I wanted.

But oh, why in my dreams
must your eyes light up
when I kiss you?
Why do you whisper soft
words of love in my ear
over and over?
Why must your arms encircle
me in their strong and
tender embrace?

And when I wake, for one
fleeting moment, I think I'm with you again.
But for just a moment
Reality returns and once again. . .
You are far from my very mind.

Tell me,

Could it all have been a dream?
Were my eyes closed
when I heard you say
those few precious words?
Had they been said too soon?
(if it were a dream, I am no longer dreaming)

Tell me,
Did I imagine the emerald of your eyes
so filled with emotion,
searching my own gray depths
for an answer or a key?
And had there been nothing there?
(if it were my imagination, my mind is blank)

Tell me,
Was I sleeping when your hands
danced across my skin
and left a burning flame
inside me. . . waiting?
And did the fire die?
(If I were sound asleep, I am wide awake)

Tell me,
Were you just a mirage in
the hot dry desert of life
just a small drop of water
from a laughing god above?
(If I were seeing things, I've gone blind)

Then I Fell Asleep

I placed my head on the soft pillow
I closed my eyes to fall asleep
I tossed and turned till I was comfortable
then I fell asleep.

I started to dream.
I saw you and me in the ocean
swimming and splashing each other.
I saw you pull me close
and kiss me on the lips.

I woke up
I sat up in bed.
Just a dream.

I placed my head on the soft pillow
I closed my eyes to fall asleep
I tossed and turned till I was comfortable
then I fell asleep.

I had longed to hold you in my arms

many nights in the past
My wish was granted, but I want something more
It's all happening too fast.

Forgive me for loving you too soon.
Forgive me for making you feel
I know that what I ask for
is too much, but only because I know
this is so real.

We're both so young and so very different
Forever may never be for us
It frightens me to fell this way
for in God I will put my trust.

I want you to love me
who knows, maybe you do
I just want to hear those words
because my Darling, I love

I've missed you my love. . .

I missed you
when I cried. . .
when I wanted nothing more
than to die. . .
when I needed someone near. . .
when I wanted someone to hold. . .
when I felt all alone in the world. . .

I missed you then but now I realize
that you never actually left.
And now that you're gone,
I don't miss you.

I know you'll never

hold this in your hands
you'll never read the words
written on this page.

For if I told you
eye to eye
that I loved you
I would never see you again.

You are so frightened of the words
that I hold so very dear

If I could only tell you

of the great fear inside
of the loneliness and heartache
that I feel
the confusion about what
tomorrow will bring.

Will it bring sunshine, flowers, rain?
Will it hold for me any special moments?
Will I find someone who'll make me
love again and know just what that word means?

Are you the one?
The one to make it all so very right?
Are you the one?
The one to make me feel and want to feel?

Will you free me of this curse upon my back?

Yes! Yes! I know you can.
I know you are the one.

If only I could sleep,

I'd dream away the loneliness
If only I could see you now
the way that I remember
If only I could press my
lips to yours
and you would respond with passion
If only I weren't so afraid. . .
of being without you

I can't really say

what must be said.
My thoughts are jumbled up,
inside my head.
They cannot come out clearly,
for you or I to understand.
But please while I try to sought them out,
hold my hand.

It's not that I don't want you.
It's not that I don't care.
It's just that there's someone else,
who I know will always be there.

Through good times and bad,
he's been by my side.
My feelings for him are something,
that I just mustn't hide.

Lately we've been fighting
and things just haven't been the same.
If I hadn't found someone else,
I would have gone insane.

I didn't plan to get so close.
I just needed a break
but now that I know you,
my feelings for him are at stake.

It was a while ago

that you loved me so.
It was a long time ago,
you wouldn't let me go.

Now it's the present time,
and you're no longer mine.
It's the present day,
"love me," you no longer say

I asked you once before

if you loved me anymore.
You said you did,
but something you hid
and left me alone to guess.

I asked do you love me
and you said yes, of course, yes.
Why don't you believe me
I'm telling the truth, don't you see.

I looked in your eyes
they were not those of one who lies,
and I believed you.
But now I know what I thought was true.

It started out as an unserious glance

in a few short weeks
it turned to romance.
I wanted him
but I had somebody else
it was so confusing
because I wanted them both for myself.
It was one of those flings
when one needs a change
but it became much more
when my feelings rearranged.
I started to need him
and just wanted him close
but it was still the same for him
because he couldn't love us both.
You see he had a girl just like my guy
we claimed to be in love with them
but still saw each other on the sly.

I never had a hand to hold

till you reached out to me
I never felt the softness of a kiss
till your lips touched mine
I never knew the pleasures of life
till you shared yours with me
I never could understand love
till you showed me what it meant.

I'm in love.

So.
But I'm in love.
So.
Really, he's special.
Yeah?
Very special.
Forget it.
No.
What?
Well Alright.

I want to be by your side

Every moment that can be spared
I want to be a part of you
and share all that can be shared
I want to whisper words of love
and hold you ever so close

In your eyes

I see a shadow
of the past
In your arms
the girl returns
of whom I thought
I'd seen the last
The wild abandonment
I used to feel
the carefree mind
the one that believed
all was unreal

I'm lost somewhere

I can't seem to find
my place in your life
As your friend
I am myself
but always yearning to
be more
to hold you close
I like this person
that I see in myself
as your friend
But yet she is always so unhappy
because she wants more
than she knows
she can have
I'm lost somewhere
I can't seem to find
my place in your life
as your lover
I cannot be all that I am
But still yearning
for it to continue
to keep holding you

I've lost myself

somewhere in the depth of your eyes
I can't seem to find
 my place
As your friend
I am myself
but always yearning
to be more
to hold you close
I see so much
that I can be
 always wanting more
than I know
I can have. . .
Because. . .
there is nothing more

I can see your face

in my mind so very clearly
not one part of you
I cannot recall
It makes it all
the harder
in this new time
another world
to keep the vow I made
the vow I must not break
for it is the only sane way out
It is so hard
because I cannot forget
or ignore
the way I'd felt in your arms
or the gentleness of your kiss
It's tearing me apart inside
because these feelings for you are so strong
You know of them
I've told you with my eyes
time and time again
and have chosen to pretend
that it's not there
And now so must I
I must hold myself back
from ever being in your presence
for every time I see your face
a golden lance pierces my heart
and every time that lance tortures me this way
another part of my very soul floats away.

1/88

I asked such a simple question

You did not understand
that all I wanted was a kiss
and the warmth of your hand

I just wanted to be held close
and reassured that you cared
I didn't ask for your love
as I know it isn't there.

Things had seemed so wonderful
almost a living dream
But now I feel as if something's gone
thus the fantasy lost its sheen

Is it my imagination
because soon I am to depart
Or is it just the simple truth
that there's no special place for me in your heart?

In your arms, I'd felt so complete
A place where I yearned to be
Did you feel the same way?
Did you yearn to be with me?

If I could only tell you

of the great fear inside
of the loneliness and heartache that I feel
the confusion of what will tomorrow bring?
Will it bring flowers, sunshine, rain?
Will it hold for me any special moments?
Will I find someone who'll make me love again
    —and know just what that word means.
Are you the one, the one to make me so very right?
Are you the one who'll make me feel
    and want to feel?
Will you free me of this curse upon my back?
Yes! Yes! I know you can
    and I know you will, my love.

I want

not what it was,
but what it could have been.

I trusted you with my secrets

and told you of my desires.
I know you heard my words,
but it's almost as if
    they we've never spoken.
For a moment in time
I touched the moon,
but now I find myself
    yearning for the closeness
    of the ground on which
    we stood.
You saw the longing in the depths of my eyes
but refused to search further
For if you did—
    is it possible that you could see inside
    and find that you have been waiting too?

12/17/87

It's been a while

since I thought of you
as anything more than a dream
I'd dreamed a night long since past
I saw you today,
and felt a queer ache in my heart
I thought it had vanished
along with the emptiness . . .
But it's still there

I'll pretend I never knew you

I'll pretend we never loved
I'll pretend.
It's so hard to pretend.

This good-bye is long overdue

It's finally time that I say it to you.
Although I know you aren't far,
I'll pretend that you're gone,
away to the stars.
I'll pretend you aren't ever coming again.
and my broken heart will just have to mend
I'll make myself believe,
    so I won't hurt anymore.

I could delude myself

and lie you
and tell you this is it.
But I know deep in my heart
that this is just not it.
I could convince myself
that I don't feel this way
    that you ignore.

I fought what I felt

But felt what I fought.

"I love you," she cried.

"*Love, you call your obsession with me, love.*
How dare you use those words?"

I wonder what it is

who it is
that you really want.
Is she all to you
that I could be?
Are the promises you make to her
ever broken,
like the promises you make me?
Your brown eyes lie,
as does my tormented heart,
for in it I cannot find strength
to let go.
I know I must,
and it must be soon,
but I cannot.
Will you grow old
with her at your side,
or is these a chance,
a small piece of your heart—for me?

I'm going to let go completely

and cease to dream these endless dreams
that have taken possession of my heart

I'm going to let go of you.
and all that might have been
for all that might have been
never existed.

Only in my mind *might have been* clung on
to the tears in my torn and tattered emotions,
for in you I saw all that I ever wanted
all that I ever needed.

I'm going to let go, as hard as it may be.
You will be far from my mind
at times when I'll wish you were by my side.

But I'll fight the urge until I have conquered
this feeling
this feeling I try so desperately
to deny
to understand
to forget.

12/22/87

I want to share my

dreams with you
my fears, my secrets
and all my thoughts too.
I want to live
in a fairytale castle,
me with my maids,
and you with your vessel.
I want to be a part of your life
     a part of it forever.
I want to belong in your arms,
     letting go never.

I've been searching

for someone special
for so long now
that I've forgotten why.
And now that I've found
someone special
I'm afraid. . .
afraid of so much
afraid to be with that someone special
    for too long.
I've forgotten what it meant
    to love and be loved
I've forgotten what it meant to be
    appreciated for who I am,
    and not what I appear to be.

I want to be by your side

every moment that can be spared
I want to be a part of you
and share all that can be shared
I want to whisper words of love
and hold you close to my breast
I want to fall fast asleep
upon your masculine chest
I want you to be my handsome hero
a prince from a place afar
I want to be your lady love
Beneath the moon and stars
I want to wander about the world
my hand clenched tightly in yours.

Lonely summer nights

by the sandy shore,
What lies ahead?
What does life have in store?
Is there a mysterious man,
someone to care?
Or is there only loneliness
Lying out there?

It started out two years ago,

when I met him at the mall.
Who would've thought it would end this way
   —with nothing left at all?

We saw each other through the winter months,
and finally fell in love in the spring
It lasted only for a short time, though,
     because *she* came along, and they had a thing.

When she dumped him,
and he didn't come back for me,
I was blinded by something
I could no longer see.

The summer was hot,
and he started coming around,
but I was wrapped up in a new romance,
someone new I had found.

Then at a party
we passed each other's way
and that's when the game
began in full play.

Weeks passed
and we saw each other more and more,
but it wasn't anything like
what we had before.

Fall came back and summer disappeared,
we'd been together for almost a year.
It would be impossible to start a new love,
because he was in between, during, and above.

We had become so close,
but there was something in the way,
our feelings had changed,
and we only knew how to play.

When it became
a year and a half,
that's when I knew
what we had was in the past.

But I couldn't let go,
we'd become dependent on one another,
yet I knew somehow
I'd have to search for others.

I knew that someday soon I had to leave
but I couldn't bring myself to believe.
So I continued to see him every other week,
sometimes we'd hold each other and not even speak.

After two years good-bye is so hard to say,
but that's what I did, when I called him today.

Little Star

Little star up above,
grant me a wish,
to have the one that I love.
Give me strength
to get through the night,
as you fly up there
like a kite.
Let me get through the day,
without tears
and without dismay.
Till I find out if you will,
I close my eyes
and my heart stands still.

My days are numbered

My life has been long
I'm packed to go with memories
here, I no longer belong.
My skin is old and wrinkled
My eyes have lost their glow
I had beauty in my younger years
but time makes them go.
I've loved and I have lost
I've hurt and I have healed
before I go you must know
that happiness is never real.
It lasts for just a moment
and as quickly as it comes, it fades
True love is just a fantasy
in this world it has no place.
Through my long life, I have searched
for something that doesn't exist
and still as I lay here about to go
the urge to find it still persists.
I am so old my bones brittle
but this long life has made me wise
What you are searching for
will never be found
so save the pain, don't cry.
Good-bye, my children.
Here there is a lesson to be learned:
Just survive—for anything more
        never yearn.

My feelings are in a turmoil

my heart has been broken in two
I know we cannot be together
and yet I'm so very in love with you.
I tried to conceal my feelings
But I know you can see it in my eyes.
My mind tells me not to worry
But my heart continues to cry.
I lied to myself a few times too many
Told myself that I truly didn't care,
for I knew that for me in your heart
there was nothing to be found there.
The days have been passing so slowly.
Your face forever looms in my mind.
Sweet solace is nowhere.
There's no escape for me to find.
I cry out in sheer desperation
for a love I know can never be,
Because, my darling,
You will never be in love with me.

Pressed Roses

We walked along the deserted lane,
you and I, hand in hand.
You leaned over to kiss me
and ah, that kiss was so grand.

You picked from a bush
these roses, so sweet,
and handed them to me
leaving our evening complete.

But now, I stare at these roses
pressed in a book.
Funny, I cannot recall your name.
Oh my, how lonely they look.

These pressed roses help me remember
that night at its best,
but I am afraid
that I have forgotten all of the rest.

Where did you come from?
What did you do
that made me keep these roses
in memory of you?

The sky is filled

with a thousand stars
there, just for you and me.
It's as if the sun appears
just so that we can see.

So many dreams I've dreamt

so many times I've awoken
I'm afraid that if I open my eyes
that the spell might be broken.
You came into my life
when I thought I was all alone.
the first gentle touch of your lips
that feeling was overthrown,
but I'm afraid that I'll awake
I'm afraid I'm seeing through mist.
I'm afraid that my dreams fade
with a farewell kiss.
I'm not too sure about how
and I don't know where it will go,
But as time passes by
my feelings begin to grow,
Life has left me fully vulnerable,
words have clouded my veins,
But even though I've heard them
I'm slowly getting to know the real you.

The right words are so hard

to come by
when one feels like I do,
In just a short time
I've found something
so special in you.

My thoughts drift to and fro
from here and to there
but they are always of you
because I've grown to care.

You're a masterpiece in my mind
outshining the sun's bright rays
there's so much I want to share
in so many different ways.

You entered my life so suddenly
bringing all that I ever wished,
the softness of your hands
and the gentleness of your kiss.

I want to let everything go
and trust you with all my fears
but it's never possible to tell
how long you will be here.

Don't promise me anything
or tell me of your fantasies and dreams
unless all that you say
is all that you mean.

And if you happen to find fault
and I'm not all that you desire
please tell me quickly
for its so very easy to fall
into the fire.

My darling, you're so very special
and deserve all that I have to bestow
and I promises my hardest to make you happy
Something I can do, I know.

So let's take it all very slowly
and see what the future has in mind.
Let's face tomorrow hand in hand
and leave all else behind.

Who knows what will happen
neither you nor I can tell what may be.
But for the time I'd like you to know
that you mean so much to me.

They Say It's Love

They say it's love
I say it's a lie,
they say it makes you laugh
when it only makes me cry.
My days are short
and my nights are long,
it's supposed to be right
but it turns out wrong.
Love for me is miserable
I say that it is dumb,
it only gets me upset
and leaves my heart numb.

To share with you

this part of my life
is the biggest joy
I can face.

To be with you
my whole life
is the biggest fear
I can face.

Through a mythical haze of blue fire

I saw you.
For an eternity, I have known you.
Your piercing aqua orbs held such warmth,
a warmth I yearned to share.
An emotion so strong so powerful,
filled my every sense.
The world seemed to cease,
leaving only two beings in its wake; you and I.
Oblivion swept away all manmade materials,
leaving us with only the moon and the stars.
Together we roamed over the highest of mountains
through the deepest of valleys.
We sailed across the largest of oceans,
on a rainbow and hiked across the never ending plains
 hand in hand, heart in heart.
With every caress, I entered a
new and fanciful universe,
my only thought of you.
Passion whizzing by like a godly comet.
Never wanting the peacefulness of our union to end,
but full of desire for the shattering conclusion. . .
And breathlessly in your arms,
I return to reality,
Only to find that when I'm in your arms,
it will always be,
one wonderful dream.

You and I are magic,

magic in its purest form
A gift of love from God above
by destiny we were drawn.

This sweetness knows no boundaries
for through space we soar
Complete and content with one another,
    needing nothing more.
Fortune has searched and found us,
we are rich beyond compare.
Together we form a golden charm
so much for us to share.

My sweet darkness pulses inside me,
an empty place of amour,
awaiting your enchantment to join me,
consuming my very core.

Always a part of one another,
no matter how far or near
Our magical love will reign forever
until the very last year.

We do not fear those coming years,
for we will be "we" in the end,
two blessed hearts entwined in love
still loving in sweet oblivion.

Your lips touched mine

but once
yet the memory forever
lingers
and my heart tingles
every time
I recall that kiss
If ever our lips
should meet again,
I'll not let go this time.

You needed me

so I cared for you,
and soon I learned to love.
As the days passed
you found that you needed me no longer.
You were able to stand on your own.
You let me go heartlessly.
I have survived,
but can no longer stand on my own.
I need you.
Can you not care for me?
You let yourself become everything to me.
And took it all away in one short breath.
You tell me to believe that
    no matter how far apart we were for now
There may always be a chance.

You slipped into my dreams

in the darkness of the night
and shed light on the most fragile
part of my person.
My hopes and desires were fruitless,
but I did not know,
for you never told me what you really were
   never told me your words were carelessly
      uttered.
I thought the world of you and you let me.
But now I see what's really inside of you;
Can admit what had been inside me
and can finally begin to forget.

Your powerful gaze met mine

I lost myself forever in a fantasy
Your lips crashed against mine
in a fiery assault
and a part of me dissolved
into the quick molten lava of your heart.
And there I burned as if in the fires of Hell
For I wanted you body and soul.
But you were the victor in every struggle
And I the conquered,
ready to be conquered again,
over and over.
In conquering me, I cursed my heart
and fought still yet another losing battle
For my heart was your prisoner
and your powerful gaze
unwilling to let go
was the captor

I cannot tear myself away

although my mind begs me to,
I cannot.
But I must.
You saw the longing
    in the depths of my eyes
but refused to search any further.
For if you did,
is it possible that you could see inside
And know that you've been waiting too?

You and I are magic,

magic in its purest form;
a match of love from clouds above.
By destiny we were drawn.
This sweetness knows no boundaries,
for through space we soar;
Complete and content in one another
needing nothing more.
Fortune has searched and found us.
We are rich beyond compare.
Together we form a golden charm;
so much for us to share.
My sweet darkness pulses inside me,
an empty place of amour,
Awaiting your enchantment to join mine;
Consuming my very core.
Always a part of one another
No matter how far or near
Our magical love will reign forever,
until the very last year.
But we don't fear those coming years,
for you will see us in the end
Two blessed hearts entwined in love
still loving in sweet oblivion

You are so very special to me

In me you've brought out things
I've never before seen.
In your arms I feel like a princess
one worthy for a throne
I shiver in your arms
when you kiss me.
suddenly I am shy
and all that I am
or was is just a shadow of the past
He, too, is special to me
but in a different way
In me he brings out things
that I thought were dead and buried
In his arms I feel like a temptress
belonging nowhere but the king's bed
I abandon all thoughts
when he kisses me
suddenly I am once again
all that I am.

You ask me from where I've come

as if I were a precious gem among stones
placed there for you to find
by a generous god.

I am not a precious gem among stones;
I am just another stone,
different in shape and size
    but a stone nonetheless.

An angelic being
    from the clear blue heavens
sent down to guard and protect
    from the harshness of life,
I am not.

I am but mortal,
with faults, with feelings.

You entered my life

by way of a dream
when I'd been searching
for someone special
and now, that I've found you
I'm frightened
of what may
or may not be
You were presented to me
a gift from a mighty God
for all of my patience
and love I need to give
And now, that I have this gift,
I'm afraid of angering
this generous God.

You again?

Yes, I remember.
You left me all alone.
I remember.
I pleaded, and I begged
What's that?
You want me back?
So sorry.
I'm *really* in love with someone now.

Your lips met mine

and I fell into a world
of fantasy verse reality.
I knew what you were.
But in my mind you were perfect.
Did I imagine things that did not exist
or did they exists but imagine me?
A wave of pleasure strong and powerful.

You come back,

but only to blow my mind away.
You leave,
    and I realize what you have done again.

You once meant

the world, my life, to me.
And, I realize now that you still do.

Start over again?

No, I don't think so.
Why?
Because from the finish line,
it's a long walk back to start

Open up the book carefully,

for the pages are yellowed
and brittle with age
It's the same story
over and over again,
page after page.
It's the story of the fair maiden
and her oh so handsome prince,
who at first detest each other
then surrender in a kiss.
It's the fantasy of the worldly knight
with those piercing blue eyes
It's so full of misunderstanding
but our hero never lies.
Her eyes shoot jeweled daggers
through his throbbing heart
but he can only admit love if they are far apart.
Milady yearns for his caress
and cries when alone
but she has too much pride
to let it be known
And only when our William steps in
and risks their silent amour
does our hero and heroine
realize what lies deep in the core
Together they fight a battle
neither knows nor understands
until the last page
when the book closes . . . hand in hand.

Mon Dieu!
(Rhapsody on a Theme of Paginini)

The music oh bittersweet music, beckoning me to
   lose myself in the rapture of its melody. Teasing
   and tantalizing crying out for me to join in its
   melancholy expressions. It warns the soul of
   life's most conflicting emotion and yet it revels
   in the splendor that only love has to offer.

Carefully, it tends to move carefully and cautiously
   down the lines of notes. Beware, it cries out
   beware that life is so often cruel in its ways.
   Beware of your heart, for in every person it lies
   within the depths of your soul. It waits to burst
   out in glorious rapture.

Do not let it frighten you for it is a gift. Take care in
   what you do with a gift so precious, so rare, or in
   only a few people does it burst out and remain.

Love . . . Yes, it is love that I see in the depths of
   your pools, calling me to join them. Yes my love.
   It is you who I love and want to share all of life's
   splendors. It is you who I want to be beside me.
   Near me. Holding me.

Do not let me go, every my love... Do not let go
ever. For without you, life does not exist. There
is nothing, no one, to replace you. You are a part
of my being. It is a love so strong and powerful
that nothing can keep us apart... Nothing!

Why after all this time is it so easy to think of you
and so very hard to forget? I know what I did
was so very wrong, but if I had known at the
time how much it would hurt being apart from
you, I would never have been so foolish.

When I lie sleeplessly in bed at night, my thoughts
drift to your familiar face, familiar now ever
though time has passed by swiftly. Your face is
before me taunting me and inviting me to share
in the very depths of you soul.

I curse myself for those insane invasions of my mind
but try as I might, they will not vanish. They
remain night after night, to haunt me and tease
me till my heart cries out in frustration. There
seems never to be a moment that your memory
does not live. Never a quiet moment that I do
not remember your dashing smile or your jade
green eyes. I've been through so much worse
than your rejection and yet it seems that I've
never been hurting more in my entire life.

Could it possibly be that I actually saw a future so
   promising withinmy reach. I believe it had been
   up to me to show you that I cared and that I
   wanted to be everything you could ever ask for.

Oh and God how I had desperately wanted to be
   everything. But somehow I was unable to be
   all of that and here I am alone thinking of your
   arms open to me, beckoning me to enter them
   and lose myself in the rapture of your embrace.
   Mon Dieu!

Why had I been so careless when all I wanted to do
   was love and be loved? Why had I let life tighten
   its strengthy grip on me and rip me away from
   the very person who could have freed me?

Even now I know the answer, but I ask myself
   over and over again, praying for some sort of
   revelation to lift this failure off my shoulders. A
   bittersweet melody floats in the background. It
   reminds me of you.

Mon Dieu!

There once was a painter who fell in love

with a painting that he had just begun to compose.
Soon after he began, he became bored,
    and the painting was left incomplete.
Set on the wall was this painting,
    new, but old to the composer.
A while passed and viewers finally
    began to see the beauty and love
    the painter had given to his painting in the
        beginning of his project.
They saw a thing of beauty—very content.

The painter then returned to the painting,
    took it down from the wall,
    and began to finish something
    that was already complete to viewers and
        the painting itself.
Once again, the painter became bored of this
        painting
    and set it back on the wall.

It was the same old familiar painting,
    but this time with incomplete touchups.
A viewer would now look at the painting
    and see questions unanswered
    no more beauty, no longer content.
Why did the painter come back and ruin a perfectly
        good thing? you may ask.
Don't ask me, darling, for you are the painter.

DARK-HEARTED SCOUNDRELS IN SETS OF TWO

I could've forgotten

but I didn't.
I wanted to forget
but I couldn't.

She is there.

I'm here.
Funny thing is you're there too.

Crying every night

is not something I look forward to.
But it is something every night that I do.

Good times:

 Some were yours.
Some were mine.
We had none together.

The dagger pierces my soul

and I want to cry out in pain
but you smother me so that
no sound comes from my mouth
I fight in vain
Your words pierce my heart
and I want to tell you of my pain
But you block out my words
so that you hear naught of what I say
I yell out in vain.

Lies

I lie in bed
thoughts of you
drift through my head
The lies you told me
all in one night
you asked me to understand
I said I might
Forgetting is hard
but forgive you, I do
because, my darling,
I'll always love you.

So, you're back again

why might I ask
I honestly don't want you
our last kiss was our last
You hurt me inside
and didn't really care
So why are you back?

What's there to say?

It's all been said,
except for what's going on
inside your head.

Your blue eyes twinkle
as if there's something behind
so tell me,
What's going on inside your mind?

Which way are you headed?

Can I follow you?
Where ever you're going,
I want to go too.

Why are you leaving?
Don't you know I'll be sad?
You're the only one I'll ever love.
The only true love I've ever had.

They tell me I can't go.
I don't understand why.
It hurts me so much,
I cannot say good-bye.

Please don't leave.
You're going too soon.
Please let me come.
I'm sure there's room.

Your face looks so pale.
Is this something you must do?
I can't live any longer.
Wait, here I come

Where are all the memories

you promised me.
Let's reminisce
about what never will be.

When time stops

that's when I'll stop.
For my mind and my soul
will never die.
I'll leave behind those
who cared for me
throughout the years
without a final good-bye kiss.

Why can't I let go

of what never was
my dreams ran away with my thoughts
and I can't find the
sanity I once possessed
for in my mind
there you live
as godly as a fierce knight
as romantic as the sweetest poet
as charming as the most handsome prince
as bold and brave as a rough pirate
And there I was in
my mind by your side
a goddess
a lady fair
a princess
a blushing maiden
All to be yours
until eternity's end.

12/21/87

You told me you don't love me anymore

I didn't want to believe you
How can this be I questioned
when only yesterday
you held me ever so tightly in your arms
In my ear you whispered words of love
and through my heart you reached my soul

You told me you've grown tired of us
I didn't want to believe you
Then I thought long and hard
You'd been gone so often
and lately we're very rarely alone
Why didn't I recognize those signs
and prepare myself ahead of time?

You told me it was truly over
love for us would never return
I didn't want to believe you.

You told me you don't love me anymore

you told me this tonight
But how can this be, when just
yesterday, you held me so very tight.
Did it ever occur to you,
how much I can hurt?
You've had plenty lessons before
because this isn't the first.
Over the phone was bad enough.

After all the love affairs

after all the tears
I still haven't learned
after all these years

Each time I think my heart has hardened
Each time I think I'll be all right
I meet the man of my dreams
and abandon my sorrowful plight

He says he'll chase away the pain
he says he'll love me always
But behind his smile and his eyes
are always hidden stories.

My eyes are sore from crying so much

these past few days because of you.
And I think to myself,
Why do I want him back if he's such an eyesore?

Just Like the Rest

I have been hurt enough
to finally know
you're just like the rest
that have hurt me so.
but all of my knowledge
and all of my pain
is not enough to keep
me sane.
I'm blinded by the charm
and the deep dark eyes
when those qualities
I should've learned to despise
My friends all call me foolish
they say I should know by now
but even after I've been through it
I still can't figure out how.
So I'm asking you a favor
please prove us wrong
Funny, now I think about it,
that's the question I've asked all along

What is it that you want from me?

Why have you come again?
To hurt me some more?
To break my heart into a million
and one pieces?
Please . . . please stay away.

Kiss me and tell me you still love me,

for I need to know if you still do.
I've done you wrong.
I know I have,
but, my darling,
I never meant to hurt you.
Our friends think you're crazy,
for even forgiving me,
but I haven't told them what
I've told you.
They haven't heard me plead.
You know I love you
and that I always will.
Please don't leave me
here in hell.

Let Me

Let me cry a while
to let out all the pain
and to add more water
to the falling rain

Let me sit alone
to calm my mind
and to add more happiness
to these horrible times

Then let me hold your hand
to let you know you're forgiven
and to add more trust
to this relationship we're living.

You were my knight in shining armor

a prince straight from a book
And in those few chapters, from me,
my heart, you took.
So godly and powerful that you were
lost was all reason
with you I was in a romance novel
filled with passion with treason.
Your eyes pierced through my very soul
in your arms I trembled
Fantasy Fiction, nothing close to reality
did "we" resemble.
Candle light, champagne,
and a few whispered words of sweetness
blinded me beyond belief
in you I saw no meekness.
Beside you I felt like royalty
a princess in a tower
rescued by a handsome pirate
filled with mischief and power.
Hot searing kisses, calloused hands
but oh so soft
In this world of fantasy
you and I got lost.
The novel was over
the last chapter to an end,
the binding has torn apart
with no hope to mend.

Don't say those words

when they mean nothing to you.
Don't tell me you care
when I know it's not true.
Don't tell me you'll be here
when I know you'll be gone.

I'll go to sleep tonight,

hoping that when I wake up,
I'll be in a different world.
I'll look upon our charade
as just another nightmare.

My heart means nothing to you.

My body you think belongs to you.
Break my heart and you will break
the binding of my person.

No longer do you hold me near

No longer do you whisper in my ear
No longer do you need me so
No longer do you let me know. . .
that you love me

Novelty

You are like a toy
all thrown out of shape
has the novelty worn away
or did you break?
Are you behind the rest of them
in a rusty old chest
can you remember
when you'd been the best?
Or is it that you were a toy
that I couldn't ever touch
sitting across the room on a shelf,
when I had loved you so much.

As I lay here alone,

all alone I hurt.
And I wonder why I've done
this to myself
I wonder why I always
come back just to be hurt.
It is no longer you,
for the things you say and do
come naturally
It is I who hurt myself
by coming back to you

Once Lovers

We were once lovers
but not anymore,
it happened too fast
and left my heart sore.
You told me you loved me,
but that soon changed
when I saw you with her,
my heart rearranged.
I remember when you said
that I meant so much to you.
How could you say that
when you loved her too?
She was far and I was near
when you were there
I dropped many a tear.
You told me you stopped
but went back often to play
Now it's only her that you love,
so you moved far away.

Or Was That Only in My Dreams

What happened to the love we had?
It seemed to just disappear
you never have enough time for me,
and I'm always left alone here.
Have you grown tired and bored
or did you forget to care?
I tried to make it work out right,
but you were never there.
What happened to those days
when you couldn't wait to call?
Now I'm sitting by my phone
and it never rings at all.
why do I feel this way,
when I promised myself I wouldn't?
I tried to fight my feelings back,
but for some reason I just couldn't.
The tears I swore would never fall
are coming down in streams.
You once were so loving
or was that only in my dreams.

It's been a long time my love

where were you when I cried?

It's been a long time, my love
where were you when I needed you?

It's been a long time, my love
where were you when I was all alone?

It's been nice talking to you
let's make it even longer this time.

To the smallest detail,

I remembered you
and was there
. . . you couldn't remember my number

You asked for nothing,
yet I gave everything, willingly
. . . and you took it all.

I wanted to be everything for you
and I was
. . . yet you didn't want me

I told you how I felt
you claimed to feel it too
. . . But your words were spoken carelessly

I wanted to be your friend
you made it too easy to
fall in love with you.
. . . and I did

These words are hard to say

when you know that you are
the only one
that feels them.
But they've been locked inside
for so very long
begging to be released.
They are not meant for your ears
for it is my secret
But this secret must escape.

There is only one

true love
There is never another one
Why is it:
Will I ever get over you?
Will I ever be free of this
spell? Will I? Will I?

The words have been

on my lips
yearning to escape
I tried to keep
my feelings
hidden far away
from your ears
for if I did not
I was so afraid
that you would get
the better of me
We argue only because
I know there is more that
there is to say.

This is the operator

May I help you?
Yes, my call won't go through.

I've been dialing his number
but I get the same answer every time.
I keep getting a busy signal.
So, is it his phone or mine?

Hold on, I'll check, so please wait.
Hurry if you will, it's getting kind of late

I'm back and it seems there's no trouble on this line
they're talking you see, so try again in some time.
Try again! I've been trying all night!
Wait a minute, something's not right.
They're talking, did you say?
and might I ask, who you meant by they?

I'm afraid I didn't ask, but I can tell you one thing
if you wait a while, his phone will ring
then you can ask him who he was talking to
But I can't guarantee he'll tell you the truth.

It's late. I'm lying here in bed.

I should be sleeping,
but too many things
are going on in my head.
Not only about you,
but about a great deal of things
and I don't know if I can cope with them.

I'm smiling now

but later I'll be crying
you won't be able to see
the hurt that you cause
... I wouldn't give you the satisfaction.

I am no longer afraid

of being hurt,
for I've been hurt already.
I'm only afraid that this hurt
won't go away.

I look into the mirror

and wonder how I've changed.
I could swear I've always looked like this.
Nothing has been rearranged.

Then I think hard
and study what's in my mind.
I could swear I've always thought like this.
There's nothing different to find.

Finally I realize that
nothing is the matter.
It's not I who has changed. . .
It's you.

Because You're Gone

I wish you came
straight out and told me
that you really didn't care,
instead of me finding out
when the two of you
were standing there.
I felt like I was invisible,
that our love never
did exist,
because you were holding
her the way
that I truly miss.
You stared into her eyes
and didn't look away,
remember when you used to
look at me that way?
I shouldn't be so upset
because life goes on,
but only for the two of you
because I can't handle your being gone.

I'll Be The One To Cry

At first it was there
a feeling of love inside,
but when you stared into my eyes
that feeling began to hide.
Where did it go?
I know it won't be back.
I loved you once, yes,
but now love is what I lack.
You're not at all offended,
'cause you never really cared,
we've grown apart
now there's nothing left to share.
Where do we go from here?
Should we just say good-bye?
I know that it's all my idea,
but I'll be the one to cry.

I'm through looking for someone

special to me,
because all my experiences
have led me to see,
there's not a guy in the world
who treats a girl right,
they only know what to do,
in the middle of the night.
They take a girl's feeling
and throw them away
and they go find another
just the next day.
They use and abuse them,
that's all they can do
and they lie when they say
Babe, I love you.
I'm through searching all over
for the perfect guy
and before I trust another,
that's the day I'll die.

I stare out my window
at the lonely street,

which is waiting for your feet
   to step upon it.

I can take it: you're leaving me.

I can take it: you're coming back.
I can't take it: you're leaving me again.

I cried hard the night you left,

and I've been crying ever since

I love you too much

to let you lie to yourself any longer.
You know you don't really love me.

If you promised me

a rose for every time you hurt me,
Sweetheart,
you'd be promising me a rose garden.

Can't we be friends?

What's wrong with just being friends?
I have someone now that I love.
A love that means so very much to me.
Well, alright.

Beck and Call

Are you at his every beck and call?
Does he do nothing and you do it all?
Do you feel like you're being used?
Are you alone, hurt, and abused?
Do you cry every night and wish he'd care?
Did he ever say please or thank you?
Would he dare?
Is he the type that will hand you a line?
Does he go out and leave you behind?
Does he pressure you into things
you do not want to do,
and do you give in just so he'll stay with you?
Does he have a heart made of stone,
doesn't care what you think, gets his thrills,
and takes you home?
Are you holding onto a guy,
who doesn't care less,
enters your life, and leaves it a mess?
I know how you feel,
I've been through it before,
say GOOD-BYE and show him the door.

He has hurt me so many times

but no more than I can take
when his heart beats next to mine
the smile I try to hide is not fake.
His hands touch my body in such a familiar
but yet so foreign to my mind
yearning for me to make him stay.
So many times, he has knocked me down
So many times, I've fallen to the ground.
No one understands why I need him so
Sometimes I feel like I don't even know.
But I try to understand his words and his ways,
that will take a lifetime so I'll take it day by day.
I'm not falling in love
that's something I learned I can not do
and if ever those three words should slip
I'll be playing someone's fool.
I know he's not only mine to hold
there are others holding him near
it hurts me to think such things
I try to fight back the fear.
I'm just an average American girl
searching for Mr. Right
but to him I'm only good enough
to hold onto throughout the night.
He has no respect for me
I can tell when he looks into my eyes
there is no way to change myself
but if I could, I'd try.
I never meant to get this close
it was just one of those things
something small got in the way
which he calls my feelings.

How could I think you were any different,

When I have been through it all before?
Why did I feel that in this instance
I could ask for so much more?

It's cold outside, the air is chilly
and it reminds me of the pain
As does the snow, the heat, the sun
and most of all the rain.

But I no longer feel that paid
of a thousand broken hearts
I only feel a numbness inside
and that's what's tearing me apart.

A numbness that tell me
I should've expected it to turn out this way, and I'm
    so sick and tired
of this game with my feelings
that more than one has played.

I wonder what it is

who it is
that you really want
Is she all to you
that I could be
Are the promises you make to her
ever broken
like the broken promises you make me
Your brown eyes lie
as does my tormented heart
For in it I cannot find strength
to let go.
I know I must
and it must be soon
but I cannot
Will you grow old
with her at your side
Or is there a chance
a small piece of your heart
for me?

Cold and Lonely

The snow is cold and lonely,
but soon it will melt
and I will have forgotten
this way that I've felt.
It falls from the sky,
harder and harder each time
and I think back to the warmth,
when you had once been mine.
The winds are blowing heavy
the sky is untruly white,
staring into this empty lie
fills my heart with fright.
But for the time the snow covers,
this white and lonely place
and until it finally melts,
my feelings I must face.

The Race

Start over again?
I don't think that's smart,
from the finish line
it's a long way back to start.
We ran our race
mostly side by side
it would have been a tie
if you hadn't lied.
The path we took was narrow and long,
till you took a detour,
a turn that was wrong.
You got to the finish line
before I got a chance
and then kept running forward,
not even turning back for a glance.
When I finally reached
the very end,
you decided you wanted to
run it over again.
But I'm too tired now,
lucky I even got to this place
Don't ask me to run it again,
get someone else to join your race.

(I Knew You'd Be Back)

You left me all alone
to hurt all by myself
(But I knew you'd be back)

So maybe he was just a rebound
someone that could take my mind
off of you for a while
that is all I wanted
(Because I knew you'd be back)

I waited and I waited
you were nowhere to be found
and so I held onto him tightly
So that he could take my fright away
(Although I knew you'd be back)

and I waited. . .
still you never showed up
so this time I held on to him
even tighter
to reassure myself that I was worth something
(Though I knew you'd be back)

Time passed by quickly
and I began to wonder what
was taking so long
So I held onto him even tighter
than I had before
Because suddenly I wanted to
(But I still knew you'd be back)

and now all my waiting
has not been in vain
I am no longer holding on to him
tightly. . .
for now I am holding on to him with all my might
(Don't wait I won't be back)

The Wrong Side

She was an average girl
from the wrong side of town
she needed love
but no one was around.
It began by a glance
just a small look,
but at the sight of him
she knew him like a book.
His body was broad
his eyes had a shine,
she knew they'd be together
in just a short time,
But he was too wrapped up
for he was a rich boy
who only thought of her
as a new toy.
A toy that could be replaced
as easily as it came
but she was sure he'd realize
that this new toy isn't the same.
She fell in love with him
but much too fast
Now she's only a memory to him
a thing of the past,
How could she expect
such a boy to be able to love?
She may come from the wrong side
but not to God up above.

I Know How To Play

What I don't know won't hurt me
So don't tell me what it is that you do,
I'm afraid of finding something out
That will risk my loving you.

The things you say and the things you do
are as different as night and day,
so listen closely
I'm telling you
That's a game I know how to play.
It's nothing new,
I've played it before
even though I know it's not right.
But I want you to know
it's still you I want to hold tight.
So remember these lines
for they are one thing that will forever be true,
Although we're both doing wrong to each other
I'll always be loving you.

In the depths of your eyes

I spy a flame
that never before lit another's
I feel a deep trust and
admiration growing
inside me for you.
Vainly I try to hold back
because so many memories ago
I stepped from behind my barrier
and fell
into the cold earth of reality.
I trusted too soon
cared too soon
loved, much too soon.
Never again,
will I step out from the wall
I've built
brick by painful brick
Each stone made by my own bare feeling
cemented together with tearful
good-byes.

The wall is too strong
but should it crack
I'll be there to hold it in place
Not even the flames you possess
can burn it down
for the flames are no more powerful
than the cold solid ice of my heart.
I swear it'll not melt.
The glistening in my eyes that
could have been for you
is now just a blank hard stare.
My heart has given up
but my mind still runs wild
with dreams that have broken me before.
I'm warning you now
although there seems to be
so much about you
that's different
I can't help but feel it'll
end the same
and you will add just one more brick,
to my wall.

I searched for you

I cared for you
I loved for you
You left for her
I cried for you
she left for him
I laughed at you.

My foolish mind;

my vulnerably empty heart
awaited my precious fantasy
to fill it with tender emotions
Blinded by my fantasies,
I did not see the true colors
of those I'd admitted
into the sacred chambers
Broken disillusioned
I vowed never to admit another
on the very day
my precious fantasy
become a reality
in you.

5/9/88

A Ray of Hope

The sun's still shining
although you're gone,
I'm all alone now
but life's still going on.
Another heart ache
some more tears,
they'll all be forgotten
in the upcoming years.
There'll be others
as many as they come,
there'll be more heartache
but yours will be undone.
A ray of hope
through the leaves of the trees,
there'll be many others
who'll love me.

Are you somewhere out there

dreaming of me
as I dream of you
night after lonely night
Are you as handsome and godly
as I imagine
and someday will you hold me
gently in your arms
and whisper words of love in my ears
Do you dream of us walking along
the sandy beach
hand in hand
And as the sun sets can't you almost
feel our lips touch softly.

What happened

to the friend I thought I had in you?
What happened to the laughter we shared
 in pairs of two?

What happened to the good days when you
 were always by my side?
Where did all the time go? Why did it pass us by?

Those times seem like dreams long since dreamt.
Tis a sad thing to say, but goodbye to my once
 close friend.

* * *

My friend I find this hard to say

but now it's time to part
the love we once had shared
has drifted from our hearts.
I will always hold dear
the memories we had shared.
I will always remember
that once you actually cared.
It upsets me to think that one
could change so much,
One who I held dear
has completely lost touch.

EVEN IN THE
DARKEST HOURS

Things are going on in my mind

and they just won't stop.
No matter how hard I try to make them stop,
    my mind takes over my will.
At one point things may seem to be just fine and
    there's nothing wrong, five minutes later all
    that has to be said is a small sentence and
    I begin to think.
I hate it. I really do. It makes me feel uneasy and
    I don't know why.
I don't know what to think.
Why does a person have to feel so uneasy and
    not know why. It's not fair.
It happens all the time to me. Why?

5/24/83

Can You Hear Me?

Can You hear me?
Can You see?
I need help
Dear God please help me.
I need to be loved.
I want someone to care
instead they only yell,
I'm scared.
No one understands
Although they think they do
I need love somehow,
especially from you.

What's wrong with you

they ask of me.
There's nothing, they say,
that they can see.

You're alright, they say,
you're all there.
As long as they can't see it,
they don't really care.

But I'm not okay.
My minds locked up.
My problems are pounding hard
and they just won't stop.

I can't handle life.
I just can't cope.
Everyone's climbing up a ladder
and I'm hanging from a rope.

The pressures building up
and holding me down
I'm losing my grip.
I'll be on the ground.

Why don't they look closer
and maybe they'll see,
that there's something inside
and it's hurting me?

Forgive Me

I'm sorry if I've hurt you
or frightened you in anyway
but life is so confusing
I didn't have strength to stay.
The problems hit me one by one
and filled up in my mind,
my problems are all gone now
but I'm sorry I had to leave you behind.
You were by me when I was sick
and kissed me when I cried,
but there were things you didn't know
things I had to hide.
Please do not miss me to much
I'm not worth the bother,
but please do forgive me,
my dear Mother and Father.

I feel confused and lonely

I find it hard to cope
as if everyone's climbing a ladder
and I'm hanging from a rope.
I can't see ahead of me
and I hate to look behind
so I'm dangling on this rope
and slowly losing my mind.

Nobody knows how I feel.

Nobody cares, they just stare
and wonder:

How can nothing ever be right
for someone like her?
She sees in a blur, and cries.

So many times, I really do feel
like I want to disappear, but instead
stay here and wonder:

why is nothing every right
for someone like me.
Why can't I see,
what this damn life is doing to me.

My eyes will not close

sleep will not come
my mind is racing
what have I done?
My heart is pounding
I can hear it in my ears
God please don't let this
be my last breath here.
It was so foolish
even I don't know why
why I did something so awful
I don't want to die.
It's getting harder to think
everything turned to black
I don't want to go,
I want to come back

When life has got you

in the grip of its palm
wiggle your way out
and sing a new song

When the sea has encircled
and swallowed you whole
splash your loudest
and wait for a boat

When the wind has knocked you down
    onto the ground
anchor yourself on a tree
and wait till it slows down

When you think life
is too hard to live
think once again and then
give it all you've got to give

This is a poem for my mother, my mommy,

the most beautiful woman in the world,
    both inside and out.
    And yet you always insisted that wasn't true.
But even when you were tired, with that fed up
    look in your eye,
and the pots were banging and clashing in my
    mind and from the kitchen below,
    You were beautiful.
And I am a part of that beauty, a masterpiece
    unlike any other,
that you and Daddy created, a part of you,
    you both gave to me,
    And I thank you.
I can feel the comforting touch of your hand and
    your warm embrace,
just as it felt when I was little, I can capture it
    in my mind,
    And feel it even now.
I remember how we used to curl up on the couch,
    and how it so effortlessly erased my fears,
and yet you did not know that just by being there
    so solid, so soothing,
    They were gone.
I didn't have to tell you, when I got older,
    all that was going on;
You helped me make the right decisions
    without even knowing,
    And I didn't let you in on it.

Some things felt too personal to discuss
    and even though I didn't share them,
I didn't have to, to be affected by you,
    and the warmth of your open arms.
    I felt your support.
And now, that I'm not there with you anymore;
with your embrace at my disposal whenever
    I need it,
    I'm missing you.
I am still the person you molded me into;
    your job was complete,
like the job of so many others throughout the
    centuries,
    But I'll never stop needing you.
I can't feel your warm hands over the phone,
    our words don't do for me,
    what just sitting beside you does.
I'm afraid of losing you, Mommy
Afraid of never feeling your hands again,
Afraid that my love for you is not as obvious
    as it feels.
    I love you, Mommy, so much.
    And, yes you are, the most beautiful woman
    in the world.

I emerged from your womb

and it was time to let go.
I took my first step without your hand,
    and it was time to let go.
I uttered my first word, however inaudible,
    and it was time to let go.

THE GUY WITH THE
CAT GREEN EYES

So Now He Dies

He was an average teen,
a youthful boy
the cruel world took over
and his life was destroyed.

His face was flushed
with every tear,
his arms were poked
with needles of fear.

He wanted help,
but no one could see
his heart yearning for love,
no one but me.

He begged and pleaded
with his eyes,
but sometimes it's too late
So now he dies.

Where Have You Gone?

I always thought of you
as a boy that could get by
on his own
but now they've taken you away
to a place that is
unknown.
I've asked everyone
where you've gone
but no one seems to care,
I only wish that someone knew
so I could get this letter there.
At night my mind wonders
about things that could've been,
before you went into your
own little world,
filled with mischief and sin.
My love, I'll try to find you
wherever you might be,
try to come back to the one that loves you,
    try to come back to me.

You're On Your Own

You'll be home again
the time's growing near
but I was wrong when I said
I will always be here.
I'm no longer yours
I'm afraid never again,
why should we go on
playing a game of pretend?
At one time I thought
you were all of my life,
but that time is gone
you didn't treat me right.
So when you're back
and in your own home,
don't bother to call me
you're on your own

You're so cruel and yet so loving

so distant and yet so near.
I need you always and forever,
yet I don't want you here.

How they did once love each other

though sometimes things change,
they were so unlike
it was strange.

They spent all hours
together of the day.
At night she'd go to sleep
and he'd be out to play.

She'd sit quietly
on the chair,
while he slowly killed himself,
without a dare.

Hurt would show
in her eyes
as he used drugs
to cover his cries.

At all times
she gave him her love
now him must give it back,
from way up above.

I overheard them talking

about who I think I know,
with every other word they said
it hit my heart with a mighty blow.
They laughed and joked
about his life
it hurt me so because
they had no right.
He never cried and never
showed his fear,
then why they said, should anyone
shed a tear?
As I looked into their eyes
with a silent stare,
I could see there was no love,
nothing. . . not there.
They went on talking about
this boy they once knew,
for they were no longer friends with him,
I wonder. . . is it you?

I can grieve for the loss of you now

Now that the worst has past
and you've ceased to care
I can grieve for the fun we had
for the quiet moments the caresses
All the things we shared
painfully now I remember
How very much we'd loved
How much you meant to me
Although I remember why you cried
and things you said
The worst is fading from my memory
I can grieve for you now
that you've finally left the world of my mind.
And once the mourning is over
It is myself that I will find.

They were just two kids,

growing up together,
exploring the life,
they thought goes on forever.

They claimed their love
was so very real,
for no one to take away
for no one to steel.

But then they said,
he was no good for her,
they took him away
and forced her to stay.

He never stopped caring
she never stopped crying
they still need each other,
and never stopped trying.

Soon years began to pass.
It was a long time,
but they found each other at last.
and they were happy.

Gone Away

He's gone away
and won't be home
he's left me here,
all alone.
He's miles away
and nowhere in sight.
he wants to be here,
so he puts up a fight.
to me he means
oh so much,
but in our letters,
we cannot touch.
His hands are laying
upon my heart,
knowing that helps me.
when we're apart.
He'll come home
and when he does,
He'll be the one,
that I'll always love.

Dream World

He lives in a dream world,
a world that's exciting
But when the music stops,
that world becomes frightening.
He's not all together
his mind's not all there
his eyes are red and bloodshot
with a vicious glare.
He pretends he has everything
except for any fears
but a night when it's quiet,
from his eyes fall tears.
He's a strange person,
So he's pushed aside
There's nowhere for him to run
nowhere to hide.
That's why I hold him
tightly I do
and say ever so softly
Babe, I love you.

From Way Up Above

They had a love that wouldn't ever change.
Their thoughts and ways were so different
most said it was strange.
Together they spent the hours of the day,
at night she'd go to sleep and he'd be out to play.
She'd sit quietly on a chair,
while he slowly killed himself without a dare.
Hurt would show in her eyes
as he used drugs to cover his cries.
At all times she gave him her love,
but now he must give it back,
from way up above.

Carefree illusions

delusive friends
it's nearing that time
time to end.
Laughing faces
tears in the mind
It's still early
but it's nearing that time.
He sits in the corner
surrounded by friends
deception, trickery, deceit
it's all just pretend.
Hey boy it's getting late
you can still make it home
I am here to help
if you can't do it alone.
Still he remains
The party going strong
whispers in the mind
of a strange sad song.
Minutes hours pass
is he really slowing down?
Why isn't he moving,
help him off the ground.
Just when he decided
it was that time to go
he was too wrapped up
just couldn't lay low.
Life was just a party
of ice and to burn
it was just a party
from which he never returned.

As I walked down the street

3 years ago today
you called me over
but I didn't stay
I continued on walking
but stopped dead in my trail
something made me want to turn around
my face turned pale
who were you, I'd seen you only
once before
You were so attractive, but there
was something more
We talked for a moment
and I knew right then and there
that someday we'd be together
we'd definitely make a pair
Things that hurt me so
soon I found out
with just a few questions
I knew what you were all about
My heart bled for you
and I wanted to help
I thought of you more
than I did myself

It is not that I don't want you

but you're soon going away
and I know he'll be here tomorrow
not only just today.
I'm so confused and feel so alone
I don't know what to do
I need him so very much
yet I still want you.
If you could just understand
these questions in my mind
maybe you can find the answer
that I need to find.
I'm not out to hurt you
I've been hurt myself before
just please realize that I want you
but I can't go on like this anymore
I need to know that if I fall in love
I won't be left behind
Can't you see all the things
going on in my mind?
It's not that I lied to you
these things at the time just didn't seem to matter
But suddenly I feel apart
my thoughts just seemed to shatter.
(unfinished)

It's Turned Into A Nightmare

You were my only dream
and that dream of mine came true
but now it's turned into a nightmare
because I've become frightened of you.

The things we had and the things we shared
are somewhere in last night's dream,
tonight's had a different story line
because I awoke from my own scream.

We still hold each other in the darkness
    of the night
but once again it ends as soon as
the sun sheds its light

We must say good-bye to each other
because the dream's coming to an end
and so I can start having peaceful dreams
    once again.

What happened to that wonderful feeling?
It just vanished it seems,
you once were so loving
or was that only just a dream?

Phone Call

I got a phone call late last night,
His voice was low and full of fright.
Nowhere to go and nowhere to turn
what will he do? when will he learn?
It was a long chase, but he got away.
He's free for a while, but where will he stay?
He asked for my help for the very first time
I told him to come home. His house or mine.
With little money and a long way to go
he started on his way back, his head held low.
Why does it seem that he just won't last?
Maybe it's because he's living life too fast.

As the train spins by

the scene outside the window
changes rapidly
as if a counterpoint of
time each moment is just
a memory
Each kiss still lingers on
my lips but it was
just another scene
to be
remembered
Nothings stays the same
the world forever
changes

I am trapped in a prison,

where walls are built of emotion,
where hearts are separated by iron
yet united in dense stone.

I am confused and alone in this prison cell.
Here I am your victim.
No fleeing frees me!
No cries release me!

My fists cannot destroy these walls
you have chosen as my home.

Feelings drift through the guarded window.
But they only reach you, my captor.
And so heartlessly you lock them away
deep within your icy heart.

Though the cell is frozen, I am warm.
I do not want to be free,
yet I do not wish to be held.

Hand me the key to my cell, precious captor, if you
    will.
You need not release me.

Just assure me that I can leave . . .
    at will.

11/85

A key to a poem.

The lock has been released
The stone walls begin to crumble.

I am free . . .

If I remain within the walls,
will I hear the echoing of the bolt
as it is being pushed back into place?
Will this chance ever present itself anew?

If I abandon this cell,
the sunshine will awaken me to a new world
void of the empty bleakness of your holding.

I may roam about the expanse
with no concern for boundaries.

Precious captor, I am remorseful
Still, I have chosen freedom.
The walls made me feel secure,
but I must find the courage to be free.

The keys are yours now,
jingling as they hang in the lock.

I have locked myself out of your prison.

12/6/85

You contend that he is my keeper.

and that I should wish to be free of him
as I wished to be free of you,
But he is not my keeper
I am his equal.

He does not confine me in a cell.
He shares me with the world, and the world
    with me.

We know of no boundaries
limiting our distance.
We are not separated but united,
in the solid stone of earth and
in the magnificent colors of
sunset.

We laugh and we love.
We do not injure one another.

I recall a time long ago
when I hurt and cried out in pain.
That cell was a world so blocked from
reality ..

This man holds no key.
He holds me to him without a lock.
To wish to be free from him
would be more foolish than to wish not to be
    free of you.

So I see you have a new victim.

A victim who resembles me.
But only in the eyes of the walls.

I pity her locked away.
For after this freedom I have seen
I would go insane in your cell.

If you mean to make me jealous,
parading her on your chain,
You cannot.
How can I envy a prisoner.

I am resentful of the warmth from deep within
that you reveal to her, however sparingly.
But what is a few moments of warmth
compared to an eternity of sunshine?

What is life when you are locked up
and afraid to see what the world holds?

What have you to offer her
besides the scenes through the guarded window?

No my once precious captor,
I do not covet what she has I never will.
My pity is my only offering to your new victim.
She is blind as I once was.

She is trapped in a prison
where the walls are made of emotion
where the hearts are separated by iron bars.

FUNHOUSE

A Dog's Prayer

I need a friend.
Will you be mine?
Will you take care of me
and be very kind?

I sit in the window.
My tail's wagging. See?
My eyes are watching you.
Please buy me.

I'll stay at your side
or curl up at your feet.
I can bark at intruders
and be rather sweet.

I won't make a mess.
I promise not to bite
and I'll try very hard
to make stormy days bright.

I need a friend.
Will you be mine?
I know you can do the job
and will do it just fine.

Don't cover me in fur

or drown me in gems
I want a single
rose
with a long green stem

Don't buy me diamonds
or a brand new car
a single red rose would be
appreciated by far

Do not bow to me as my subject
 no crown upon my head,
just present me with a single rose
of deep deep red

Do not give me candies
no cherries covered in sweets
just a simple red rose
would be much of a treat

Don't shower me with exotic flowers
I'm a plain and simple girl
who could use one red rose
in this material world

A rose is from the heart
red represents a certain way
a single one means love
so present me with me this day.

I can't sit here

staring at the clock.
I gotta think quick
and get around this mental block.

Everyone's finishing
and I'm gonna faint.
What happened to the good old days
when final exams were done with finger paint?

Wait, hold it
I can see,
the person's paper'
in front of me.

Answer 2 is number four.
Damn, my pencil just fell on the floor.

What's this?
A cheat sheet under my desk.
I just might end up
passing this test.

Oh no, here comes my teacher.
I might end up being this afternoon's feature.

Great she just passed me by.
This is the wrong cheat sheet.
I think I'm gonna die!

I knew I should've studied harder.
Now I'm gonna get it from my father.

There's just a couple more minutes
then I can finally rest,
but what am I gonna do,
if I fail this test?

I should've got more sleep.
I'm really tired.
What's this, I hear?
Hey man, the school's on fire!

Life guards yell,

are ya listening?
On the beach,
the sand is glistening.
In a beach bum way,
we're happy today. . .
lying on a very sandy beach.

In the summer we can go a surfin'
and pretend the waves are oh so big.
They'll come splashing down and we'll say,
    "Wow man then we'll fall asleep.

The Hair Cut

I showed her the picture
and said, "exactly the same"
I put all my trust in her
and didn't even know her name
How foolish I was
to sit there so quiet
I could've gave her some tips
but I was too tired
I watched through the mirror
while she snipped away
I closed my eyes
and began to pray
That's it she said
As I opened my eyes wide
She stood behind me
glowing with pride
Hold it a second
It's not there
Hey lady, I trusted you
Now where's all my hair?

No heat! No hot water!

What praytell, is up with the boiler?
A window is loose,
the ceiling is down,
How come the super,
is never around?

The faucet is leaking,
the rent is too much
the tub is stopped up,
the toilet won't flush!

The paint is chipping,
there are holes in the walls
the roaches are advancing
there's garbage in the halls!

The electricity is out,
a work crew is needed
the pipes are gushing water,
the repairs are never completed.

The locks are too flimsy,
the doors are not secure,
Every time I take a shower,
there's a flood on the floor.

The rain water is leaking
upon my bed,
I fear that the ceiling
shall fall upon my head!

The gas has been shut off,
I can't cook my food,
the fridge door won't close,
the repairmen are rude!

The radiator in the small bedroom,
is ruining the carpet,
the water is constantly running,
and I just can't stop it!

I've exhausted your patience
you've exhausted mine,
Eviction is scheduled shortly,
    I hope to skip out in time!

The Hips

Twas the night before Easter and all through the tent,
    all the hips were smoking pot, because they gave
    cigarettes up for lent.
The marshmallows were roasting by the fire with care,
    in hopes that romping rabbit would soon be there.
Tuff tweaty and sweety were rearranging their nest,
    while Stoned Stanley and Stephi were having
    some s**.
High Hilda in her bandanna and Hari in his vest had
    soon settled down to give it their best.
When out in the woods, there arose such a moan
Hari sprang from his bag and went to get Stoned.
Away to the woods, Stanley and Hari did fly,
    approaching the bushes that seemed to groan
    and cry.
When what to their wondering eyes should they spot,
    but Rough Ruth and Junki Joni all sweaty and hot.
They couldn't hold it in any longer watching Joni jiggle,
    they looked at one another and started to giggle.
Junki Joni got up and started off by calling each one
    a f**k.
"You're a dip! You're a dick! You're a prick and a f**k.
    Next time you do it, I hope it gets stuck!"
At the top of their lungs, all choked up with laughter,
    they let it all out, faster and faster.
As Rough Ruth went on giving Joni a blow,
bothersome bee flew by and hit Hari in the nose.
So back to the Tent, Hari and Stanley did walk,
    to Hilda and Stephi, but not to talk.

Within a second they hear on the tent,
   Wacki Wanda and Waisted Willi, using time
   well spent,
and as Hari stuck his head out and was looking around,
down came Wanda on top of him with a bound.
She was dressed in nothing but a single shoe
   and Willi in nothing but a bandanna that was blue.
Hari's clothes were in a pile on top of his boots
aside of them was a bag full of leuds.
Hari's eyes were covered in a pair of dark shades
and so were the rest of the Hips, in case of a raid.
Hari had a little mouth of which Hilda was fond
   and the beard on his chin was dirty blond.
The butt of a joint, he held tight in his teeth
   and the smoke it encircled Hilda's tit, like a wreath.
Stanley had a hairy face and a little round belly,
   due to the fact, he liked strawberry jelly.
Stephi was skinny, a voluptuous slut,
   her pastime was nothing, but a mere little f**k.
With a wink of her eye, Ruth saw Hilda giving Hari head,
   soon gave her to know, she had nothing to dread.
The Hips said nothing, but went on with their folly,
   while Funki Fido rolled over in the Freadas of
   the Valley.
Everything was quiet in the Hip Territory that night,
   mainly because they were all wrapped together
   tight.
They fell asleep on the cold ground soon
under the stars and the shimmering moon.
But Hari did say, before he fell fast asleep,
   "Hilda, I love you."
There was not another peep.

FOREVEREVER LOVE

**With black lashes resting soundly
against ivory cheeks,**

I began to dream.
A man appeared from out of the mist,
mysterious he seemed.
A rose silently boasting its delicateness,
in his strong hand, he held.
I was afraid to touch it, for my warmth
would cause it to melt.
My bare skin tinged with warm desire
and I relaxed in blue haze.
No modesty felt, as I boldly awaited his touch to
    replace his gaze.
The man came close; his lips descended;
we met in a shattering kiss
. . .my fingers nearly touched the rose,
as it vanished into the mist.
So my hands caressed the soft skin
of his golden muscled back.
He turned slowly around and my wet lips trailed
    down
the previous track.
I kissed his back until it tingled
his skin glowing like coals,
then he lifted me into his arms
and carried me in his tender hold.
A soft cloud of dove feathers lowered for us
    and he gently laid me down
my hands reached to him
his golden lance I found.

I wanted to give him pleasure and
proceeded to do just that.
He filled me with an intensity and
there was nothing I'd hold back.
And before his passion was spent
his hands on my should asked me to cease
He joined me on the soft dove feathers
more pleasure before our release.
And when neither of us could wait anymore I
    lowered upon his shaft
Our eyes met, our hearts pounded;
each breath we thought would be our last.
The feelings were so overwhelming,
through our veins and in our mind
The ultimate surrender was our reward
for a love so hard to find.
A part of one another now
for an eternity, one we would be
I proclaimed undying love and
he the same to me.
I needn't fear that I would wake
and put an end to this beautiful scene
for the special man in my life
is the same man from this dream.

My darling,

there's a deep love inside me,
growing each new day
I want you to know how very much,
but I've run out of words to say
Help me my sweet to express the powerful
feelings gathering inside
Help me let you know of my love that
has reached higher than the sky
With my pen upon this paper, I imagine
you, close and so clear.
Although my arms were around you yesterday
Oh God, now I wish you were here
There are no words that can describe the beauty
I see so clearly in you.
You're Apollo from the heavens; a handsome
      prince worldly knight; a Greek statue.
I want to hold you in my arms and be
for you all that I can
I want to be your wife; your mistress;
your sweetheart; your best friend.
You're so very special, a gift you must be from a
      generous God above
For this happens only once in a lifetime,
our very special love.
I'll love you forever, my darling and never
shall it cease
My love for you will keep on growing
tomorrow and for all eternity.
I love you.

So very new—

precious youth
innocence lost forever
in a swirling sea of passion
no path home
no way back to the beginning
drowning in bliss
suffocating—
slave to love
unrequited
silently slip out
in the darkness
don't look back
until the door is closed
a key binding it shut
for eternity
search for the piece
of your missing puzzle
out there
somewhere
close by
and swim to
the edge of life.

2/4/88

I've been wandering aimlessly

through a daisy-filled meadow.
I pluck one of the white and yellow flowers
    every so often
    and bask in its fragrance
    —eventually, it wilts.
    —it lies limp in my hand.
So on I wander,
    leaving the daisies
        rooted safely to the earth
            —myself, protected.
I glimpse a rare flower
    so bright, so extraordinarily beautiful.
    I lean over and touch it
        ever so gently with my
            fingertips.
I do not wrench it
    from the ground
        I enjoy its fragrance
        from where it stands proudly
        —it brings me
            ultimate joy.

3/88

Memories are a thing of the past.

Learn from the bad memories
and think often about the good memories.
And never stop making memories.

The Poetic Stranger

My day at work was long and hard,
the train was a moment away.
As the doors opened, I shuffled in,
to end this dreary day.
I curled up in a corner seat,
my ticket in my hand,
but before I drifted off to sleep,
I spied a handsome man.
He settled down beside me
and lost himself in black and white.
I felt secure and comfortable
so sleep, I did not fight.
I slept away the tension
with the poetic stranger at my side,
I dreamt of a knight in shining armor,
a hero from another time.
He was there beside me,
when my eyes opened to the light.
I could see his reflection in the window
blocking out the darkness of the night.
In his strong hand he held
an index card—words written in blue,
he leaned over and gave it to me
and said, "This poem is for you."
In a moment he was gone
through the closing doors of the train.
I stared at the words before me
and wondered from where he came.
His poem was sweet and sensuous,
I swore I was still asleep,
dreaming up this prince charming,
with thoughts so sensitive and deep.
From this romantic dream,
I didn't want to wake
afraid of never seeing him again,
yet afraid my heart he'd take.
On a train bound for home,
a poetic stranger entered my life,
although it sounds so unreal,
it seems to be just right.   2/20/88